Th
Of

Joseph Gelfer

SUMMERSDALE

Copyright © Summersdale Publishers Ltd, 2002

No part of this book may be reproduced by any means, nor transmitted, nor translated into a machine language, without the written permission of the publisher.

Summersdale Publishers Ltd
46 West Street
Chichester
West Sussex
PO19 1RP
UK

www.summersdale.com

Printed and bound in Denmark
by Nørhaven Paperback A/S, Viborg

ISBN 1 84024 269 8

Cover illustration copyright © StiK, 2002

Contents

Essential CV Tips	4
At The Interview	8
What Do Your Office Clothes Say About You?	20
Ingratiate Yourself Quickly	30
Get Wise To Office Tricks	41
Understand The Strange Dialect of Management Speak …	49
When It All Starts Getting Too Boring	61
The Office Party	71
How to Throw the Perfect Sickie …	81
Office Archetypes	88
Office Sexual Relations	96
What the Drinks Machine Says About You…	100
When it's Time to Find Another Job	106
How to Get the Sack	118

THE LITTLE BOOK OF OFFICE BOLLOCKS

Essential CV Tips

The first step to getting that coveted office job is writing your CV. But how to make that first impression count?

Don't leave marmite smudges on your CV.

Don't print your CV on Spider-Man stationery.

Don't include your Scout or Guide leader for a reference.

ESSENTIAL CV TIPS

Think of the things that you're good at and work them to your advantage on your CV:

I enjoy shopping
= I have brand awareness

I play five-a-side football
= I am a team player

I like gambling
= I am an educated risk taker

I am promiscuous
= I am a people person

I am lazy
= I am thorough

THE LITTLE BOOK OF OFFICE BOLLOCKS

Don't fill in the application form with **green** or **lilac** ink.

Don't sign your name with hearts and kisses.

Get a decent e-mail address, i.e. *not* wild_stallion@hotmail.com.

Never use exclamation marks in your covering letter! And NEVER EVER use multiple exclamation marks and lots of CAPITALS!!!!!

ESSENTIAL CV TIPS

Make sure you understand what the job advert actually means:

executive	=	assistant
entry-level	=	badly paid
graduate	=	no experience
mature	=	elderly
young	=	pretty
flexible	=	door mat

THE LITTLE BOOK OF OFFICE BOLLOCKS

At The Interview

Brush up on these handy phrases to cover up the truth.

'I am very confident at finding my way around a computer'
I know how to delete naughty pictures from the Temporary Internet Files cache.

AT THE INTERVIEW

'In my previous position I felt I played a crucial role in improving team morale'
I made all the tea and was the butt of everyone's jokes.

'I have a strong grasp of a wide range of e-mail packages'
I can e-mail ten friends a day as well as using Instant Messenger and ICQ.

THE LITTLE BOOK OF OFFICE BOLLOCKS

'In my previous position I enjoyed being a team player in facilitating inter-office communications'
I went to the post box at 5:15 every afternoon and circulated the office memos.

'I like to think I cope well with potentially difficult people'
Give me the job and I won't complain when you're mean to me.

AT THE INTERVIEW

Anticipate some classic interview questions – and never answer with the truth:

What do you feel you could bring to this company?
An exceptionally organised approach to my duties (NOT *My collection of fluffy pigs which I intend to smother my desk in*).

THE LITTLE BOOK OF OFFICE BOLLOCKS

What is your strongest personal attribute?
Strong attention to detail (NOT The ability to drink ten pints of lager without spewing).

What is your weakest personal attribute?
That would probably have to be my need for everything to be perfect (NOT I find it very hard to work more than two weeks without a sick day).

AT THE INTERVIEW

How would you deal with a conflict situation?
It is very important to see all sides and not to deny a person's experience (NOT I'd shout at them with a raised fist until they saw my point of view).

THE LITTLE BOOK OF OFFICE BOLLOCKS

Be sure to make up interesting facts around the following themes:

team sports

international travel

scuba diving

voluntary work for the community

AT THE INTERVIEW

Imagine all the interviewers are sat on the toilet having just run out of loo paper. You have the loo paper and they want it.

Flirt just enough for the interviewers to think they might get lucky at the Christmas party, but not so much that they think you'll have a go with everyone in the office.

THE LITTLE BOOK OF OFFICE BOLLOCKS

Wear some naughty underwear so you feel you know something that they don't. Give the impression to the interviewers that you might be wearing some naughty underwear too.

AT THE INTERVIEW

Let it slip that from time to time you have been known to go out with friends and 'have a few drinks'. Then chuckle knowingly with the interviewer. Everyone likes a person who'll be the first one to suggest going down to the pub and then sinking a few.

THE LITTLE BOOK OF OFFICE BOLLOCKS

Imagine you're all wearing togas. Notice how your toga is that bit smarter than theirs.

Be protective about your briefcase as if there is something very important inside it.

AT THE INTERVIEW

When shown to the desk for an IT test, chuckle out loud and say, 'Wow – I haven't worked on one of *these* for a while.' Then refuse the offer of a coffee, giving the impression you drink nothing but water or herbal tea during the day.

THE LITTLE BOOK OF OFFICE BOLLOCKS

What Do Your Office Clothes Say About You?

When you walk into the office for the first time, take a good look at what your co-workers are wearing. It's amazing what you can deduce about people's personalities from their clothes.

WHAT DO YOUR OFFICE CLOTHES SAY ABOUT YOU?

Sharp suits: 'Keep an eye on me or you'll regret it.'

This is an obvious power freak, liable to go mad at a moment's notice. They are likely to be a uniform fetishist, and still living with mum (free ironing). They are probably hiding a spindly physique and tend to be manipulative.

THE LITTLE BOOK OF OFFICE BOLLOCKS

Crumpled suits: 'Trust me with your secrets.'

Someone who wears a crumpled suit is likely to be a creative, easy-going, family person, lacking in confidence. Also likely to be a secret weed smoker who will tell you whatever you want to hear for the easy life.

WHAT DO YOUR OFFICE CLOTHES SAY ABOUT YOU?

Cargo pants: 'I'm just *so* approachable.'

Ah, the trendy try-hard. This person is likely to be approaching middle age, and a DIY expert who's scared of getting old.

High heels: 'Come on in boys – watch out girls.'

Well, it's obvious isn't it? Kinky, exciting, power hungry, a Dallas and Dynasty fan. If it is a man wearing high heeled cowboy boots or similar, watch out – this guy is a seriously insecure exhibitionist. Or maybe he's just short.

WHAT DO YOUR OFFICE CLOTHES SAY ABOUT YOU?

T-shirts and trainers: 'I'm just *too* radical for this office.'

Young and energetic surf or skater type; gay (if tight T-shirt); bound to be passed over for promotion. But hey, they don't care: they just want the money for lost weekends.

Jumpers and cardigans: 'I've been working here so long, no one will suspect me of doing anything naughty at all.'

Past caring thinking about clothes. A curtain-twitcher, possible gossip, and probably a frustrated history teacher. But looks can be deceiving: this person may well be wearing a basque under that cardie – yes, even if he looks too broad for one.

WHAT DO YOUR OFFICE CLOTHES SAY ABOUT YOU?

Chinos: 'It doesn't bother me that I'll never progress beyond deputy manager – it is a very fulfilling position.'

Loves shopping at Burton, misguidedly assumes trendiness.

THE LITTLE BOOK OF OFFICE BOLLOCKS

Hats: 'Look at how astonishingly individual I am!'

Generally mad.

Jeans: 'Look how unconventional I am wearing jeans to the office!'

Drainpipes	= Def Leppard fan
Stonewashed	= Essex girl/boy
Twisters	= fashion victim
Marks and Sparks	= soon to retire
Generic cheap brands	= already married

WHAT DO YOUR OFFICE CLOTHES SAY ABOUT YOU?

Comedy ties and socks: 'Look at me, the comedy genius!'

Desperately trying to appear fun but not brave enough to wear hats, despite thinking they're really cool. Liable to say 'D'oh!' like Homer Simpson every few minutes. Their desk will be covered in small toys with springs and their computer will make a string of comedy sounds every time an e-mail arrives.

A blue gingham tabard and wrinkly tights: 'I am the cleaner.'

THE LITTLE BOOK OF OFFICE BOLLOCKS

Ingratiate Yourself Quickly

If you want to make a good impression from Day One, follow these simple tips that will set you up for success.

Make an Excel spreadsheet of the office's tea and coffee tastes, showing suitable technical know-how and willingness to put the kettle on at the same time.

INGRATIATE YOURSELF QUICKLY

Ask the boss where they got their shoes from as you've been after a pair just like them for ages.

Pretend to have a heavy cold but refuse to go home saying you want to get the work done. Make sure people notice you taking medication, wincing at headaches and clearing vast amounts of sinus blockages.

THE LITTLE BOOK OF OFFICE BOLLOCKS

Show sophistication through disdain of instant coffee and tea with sugar. Never make your sandwiches with white bread – it's an invitation for ridicule.

Express your dissatisfaction about other people's laziness to the boss. Never name names but make it quite clear who you're talking about.

INGRATIATE YOURSELF QUICKLY

Become well versed in the Boss's favourite soaps and TV dramas and make sure you like the same characters that they do.

Make sure the security staff know your name so people think you're more important than you actually are.

Pretend the computer has just wiped a whole bunch of work. Smile, shrug your shoulders and say, 'Oh well, best just do it all again.' People will think you have a superb attitude and then you can waste the next however many hours playing free cell and solitaire.

INGRATIATE YOURSELF QUICKLY

Conspire with your boss in arguments they have with their partners on the phone and encourage them to moan about it, taking you into their confidence. Leak rumours about the content of those arguments with your co-workers in exchange for information on other people.

Conspire with your boss when they moan about their workload and the amount of responsibility they have. Say you're so glad you don't have to deal with all the hard work the managers have to contend with. Say, 'I don't know how you do it' and smile sympathetically.

INGRATIATE YOURSELF QUICKLY

Having soup for lunch makes you look like a good person. Having low-fat soup makes you look like a saint.

Have flowers delivered to yourself at work so everyone else thinks you are incredibly popular.

Familiarise yourself with the managers' birthdays and arrange a collection. You will look good to the manager, who will inevitably find out, and encourage others to give more money when your birthday comes around.

INGRATIATE YOURSELF QUICKLY

Comment on how cool the boss's new mobile phone is and ask where they got it. Pretend you're interested in their comments about the right type of contract to opt for. Pretend to be interested in their theories about what a person's ring-tone says about them.

THE LITTLE BOOK OF OFFICE BOLLOCKS

Support the local football team – everyone likes an underdog.

Always be nice to the cleaner as they're probably the only person in the building earning less than you.

Get Wise To Office Tricks

Here are a few tricks every office worker should know ...

Pretend you're naive. Having everyone else think you're a bit stupid is one of the most powerful office positions to occupy.

THE LITTLE BOOK OF OFFICE BOLLOCKS

Always make sure you're connected to a superior printer than everyone else on the same grade as yourself.

Always double the amount of time you expect a task to take if a superior member of staff asks. You can then either take is easy or impress them by doing it faster.

GET WISE TO OFFICE TRICKS

Under no circumstances admit to walking in to work. You can then blame any lateness on the bus or train. Also, when the inevitable transport strike hits you will be able to either a) say that you're unable to make it in today because of the strike; or b) say you will come in *despite* the strike, but secretly have no hassles. Either way you come out on top.

Never let it be known that you know how to do something unless you're happy to be the person who does it regularly.

Make yourself a minority member of society. Coming from a difficult background, or having dyslexia and trying your best in the face of adversity, makes it much harder for the boss to give you any grief.

GET WISE TO OFFICE TRICKS

Be religious – this makes it harder for people to be nasty to you.

Never water plants – if you do you will get the blame when they eventually die.

Keep a spreadsheet of all the porkies you told at the interview so you won't be caught out in the future.

Resist the temptation to only be friends with the cute members of the office – plain people are often more powerful.

GET WISE TO OFFICE TRICKS

Never take responsibility for the air conditioning or you will be to blame when some people are too cold and others too hot.

Never take responsibility for the alarm system or you will end up being the first in to work and the last out, as well as the people the police call in the middle of the night when it eventually goes on the blink.

THE LITTLE BOOK OF OFFICE BOLLOCKS

Never talk about existentialism – no one likes a wet blanket or wants to hear about something they don't really understand.

Never comment upon Health and Safety regulations or you will be forced to become the Health and Safety Officer.

Understand The Strange Dialect of Management Speak …

Keep these handy translations near you at every meeting.

'That is indeed very interesting.'
There's no chance this is going to happen.

THE LITTLE BOOK OF OFFICE BOLLOCKS

'We have a real live opportunity here.'
You have a serious problem on your hands.

'Don't think I don't appreciate your contribution on this matter.'
Your work on this has been of no use whatsoever.

UNDERSTAND THE STRANGE DIALECT OF MANAGEMENT SPEAK

'I'd really value your input on this.'
I want someone else to blame when it becomes apparent I had no idea what I was talking about when suggesting this.

'We have to put our marketing hats on.'
We have to start telling more sophisticated lies.

THE LITTLE BOOK OF OFFICE BOLLOCKS

'Are we not over-egging the pudding?'
This is turning into complete bollocks.

'Let's see if this idea has legs.'
Let's see if you can turn this lame idea of mine into something workable.

UNDERSTAND THE STRANGE DIALECT OF MANAGEMENT SPEAK

'This situation requires some Blue Sky Thinking.'
Let's waste time making stuff up that's never going to happen.

'As employees we want you to establish a healthy work/life balance.'
As employees we want you to work harder.

'We want our employees to be able to work more flexible hours.'
We want you to work longer hours.

'Take pride in your work.'
Work harder.

UNDERSTAND THE STRANGE DIALECT OF MANAGEMENT SPEAK

'We need to expand our brand awareness.'
We need to convince more people of our lies and nonsense.

'This is an ideal opportunity for the company to change direction.'
The company is going under.

THE LITTLE BOOK OF OFFICE BOLLOCKS

'There has been a paradigm shift in the company's current policy.'
There has been a U-turn in the company's current policy.

'We cannot measure success by profit alone.'
We're going broke.

'We need to popularise our image.'
We need to come over trashier.

'We have to understand how our customers think.'
We have to be more devious.

'We are all going on a team-building exercise.'
We will beat the attitude out of you one way or another.

'This project has been given a green-light.'
This is a very dull idea that we are attempting to make sound more dynamic.

UNDERSTAND THE STRANGE DIALECT OF MANAGEMENT SPEAK

'We anticipate a short-fall.'
Start looking for a new job.

'At this point we are unable to offer the workforce a pension plan.'
We have spent all the available money on establishing our own private pension plans.

THE LITTLE BOOK OF OFFICE BOLLOCKS

'The company has to economise.'
You have to take a pay-cut.

'It has been brought to our attention that …'
Someone has grassed you up.

When It All Starts Getting Too Boring

It won't be long before it's 9.30 a.m. on your first day and the novelty of your new office job has worn off. Don't worry – with a little imagination you can while away the hours until the weekend.

Grow cress in your drawers.

Sign off all your e-mails, 'As Basil Brush would say – Boom Boom!'

THE LITTLE BOOK OF OFFICE BOLLOCKS

Walk around the office using only dolly steps.

Sing a show tune every time you open a new file.

Make balls out of rubber bands.

WHEN IT ALL STARTS GETTING TOO BORING

Tell everyone you're going to the toilet over the announcement system.

Make paper aeroplanes containing bizarre messages and throw them to random workmates.

Tell the boss you can't possibly work without having pets in the office.

THE LITTLE BOOK OF OFFICE BOLLOCKS

Collect bagfuls of those little paper circles that collect in the bottom of hole-punches.

Make a chain out of paperclips which reaches all the way around the office.

Suggest a cucumber-eating competition.

WHEN IT ALL STARTS GETTING TOO BORING

Wind your seat down as far as it goes and complain that the desks are too high.

Siphon off your boss's petrol into a can which you can bring out of the boot of your own car, thus saving them from what would have been inevitable disaster.

Suggest a 'pyjamas and nighties' day at the office. People will think you are a pervert and like you all the more for it.

Feign an interest in astrology, thus justifying time off most weeks to read the stars of all the interested parties in the office (this can take a lot of time).

WHEN IT ALL STARTS GETTING TOO BORING

Fabricate repetitive strain injury in order to receive lighter, less tedious, duties.

If you've been underperforming in your duties, ask for an appraisal – this initiative neutralises all your previous inadequacies.

Encourage others to have cigarette breaks, saying you've just given up. When they've gone, call up your mates on their mobiles.

Leak information that states your ideal future revolves around being a massage therapist. Paranoid members of the office will then think you are not the threat they thought you were. Others will think there's something kinky about it and think better of you.

WHEN IT ALL STARTS GETTING TOO BORING

Suggest a corporate anthem and offer to spend (i.e. waste) a day writing the lyrics for it. If you're musical you might even be able to swing a week to pen the tune.

Pretend you smoke to gather intelligence at fag breaks. Then give up, thus having an excuse for being miserable for months to come.

Encourage your co-workers to confide in you but tell them nothing in return.

Encourage your co-workers to be on the fiddle in order to mask your own, more subtle, fiddles.

The Office Party

Office parties are about as fun as seeing how many paperclips you can fit on your tongue, and there is a certain protocol you should follow if you want to keep your job next year.

Photocopy your bum. Distribute the copies to everyone you can find.

Snog the youngest person in the office.

THE LITTLE BOOK OF OFFICE BOLLOCKS

Snog the oldest person in the office.

Stand on the table and expose your underwear while singing Kylie songs.

Send the boss arsey e-mails from other people's computers.

THE OFFICE PARTY

Reprogramme the fax header to say something rude.

Renumber the managers' phone extension to pick up all the calls from reception – they'll never know how to change it back and will look daft when they have to ask someone how to fix it.

Tell about all the lies you came up with at the interview – let others tell their lies and then pretend you were only joking.

Get so drunk you start crying.

Get so drunk you tell everyone how much you love them.

THE OFFICE PARTY

Piss in a pot plant.

Create a project plan setting out how much booze should be drunk throughout the duration of the party and by whom. If people do not keep up to speed, reprimand them in the same way the project manager does at meetings.

THE LITTLE BOOK OF OFFICE BOLLOCKS

Get out the portfolio of saucy photos of yourself which you have been hiding in your bag and show them to everyone.

Supply and snort vodka jellies.

Insist on starting a conga.

THE OFFICE PARTY

Sing 'I Will Survive' at the top of your voice when it comes over the speakers.

Set the boss's screensaver to say things which question his or her sexual morals.

Change the passwords on your co-workers computers.

THE LITTLE BOOK OF OFFICE BOLLOCKS

Bring a Polaroid camera and suggest a 'guess whose bum' competition.

Employ the old 'Clingfilm over the loo seat' gag and see who comes out of the toilet with splattered clothing.

Fill an old water-cooler bottle with vodka and tonic and forget that it'll need changing before the next work day.

THE OFFICE PARTY

Spike the drinks of boring people who don't drink enough – all must be made to make fools of themselves if you are.

Put snails all over the boss's desk.

Use the CD drawer on your computer as a pint holder.

THE LITTLE BOOK OF OFFICE BOLLOCKS

Moon the management from the street through the office window.

Show what a fantastic dancer you are by pretending to be one of the Village People: Y – M – C – A.

Expose that incredibly embarrassing tattoo you had done whilst on holiday in Ibiza in 1998.

How to Throw the Perfect Sickie ...

Always set up a sickie by complaining about feeling a bit unwell a day or so before your intended bunk-off. Nothing looks more fishy than a sudden illness.

Always take a sickie when the boss is on holiday.

Set up imaginary distant relatives with serious illnesses so that you can kill them off at a later date. Use these opportune deaths to generate a funeral to cover much-needed days off.

HOW TO THROW THE PERFECT SICKIE ...

Sickies taken mid-week are less obvious than those taken on Mondays and Fridays. If you have taken a sickie on a Friday make sure to say how miserable and poorly a weekend you had in order to take the heat off a bit.

THE LITTLE BOOK OF OFFICE BOLLOCKS

Set up the occasional doctor's appointment a month or so in advance in the office diary, thus earning yourself a banked lie-in.

HOW TO THROW THE PERFECT SICKIE ...

If you've been out all night during the week, tell the office you're sick via e-mail. The message will show it was sent at 5am, showing you were up early, but that you just felt too sick to speak.

THE LITTLE BOOK OF OFFICE BOLLOCKS

Get your Mum to call in sick for you – Mums never lie.

Go out on a bender the night before you are due back to work so you look suitably haggard after your time off sick.

HOW TO THROW THE PERFECT SICKIE ...

Make extraordinary heaving sounds in the toilet so the boss sends you home.

Sniff onions to make yourself more snotty and teary before calling in sick.

Office Archetypes

The Expert: Always on hand to show you how to do anything from connecting a printer to dumping your partner. You will notice this person rarely has their own printer or partner.

OFFICE ARCHETYPES

The Nerd: Dressing like a geography teacher isn't such a crime. The butt of everyone's jokes, the nerd often enjoys the secret friendship of some of the most powerful people in the organisation. The nerd will end up the richest person in the office.

THE LITTLE BOOK OF OFFICE BOLLOCKS

The Flirt: Everyone loves the attention of the flirt, although no one really wants to be connected with them. Best avoided until the final weeks in the job - then call their bluff in the stationery cupboard.

OFFICE ARCHETYPES

The Keener: The keener is always volunteering to do the things other people don't want to do – their secret is they never actually do what they're being keen about. Best of both worlds!

THE LITTLE BOOK OF OFFICE BOLLOCKS

The Spy: Often confused with The Keener, the spy is smiling because he is feeding information back to the boss, happy in the knowledge that he will progress through the ranks without having to do much work.

OFFICE ARCHETYPES

The Gossip: Always whispering around the drinks machine. This person is a waste of space for the office, but must be kept on good terms at all costs due to their dangerous and volatile nature.

The Lad: Always hung over in the morning and then planning a night out in the afternoon. Stories of last night's conquests make people laugh, but everyone's glad they don't share a house with him.

OFFICE ARCHETYPES

The Old Fogey: This person's been working for the company since 1981 and was old when they got the job. Incapable of doing anything other than sums when there's a power cut, the old fogey remains a crucial part of any operation.

THE LITTLE BOOK OF OFFICE BOLLOCKS

Office Sexual Relations

Sexual relationships within a company can be as complex and impenetrable as middle management. Follow these rules and you should be fine ... just keep your options open, eh?

Only flirt with people whose partners are smaller than you.

OFFICE SEXUAL RELATIONS

Never flirt with a single person unless you're willing for them to call your bluff.

E-mail flirts are less dangerous than verbal flirts.

Learn the art of ambiguity to avoid recriminations.

Never totally reject flirts from the boss.

Gay flirts are safer than hetero flirts and nearly as fun.

THE LITTLE BOOK OF OFFICE BOLLOCKS

Only every expose the top half of your underwear during office hours.

Sucking fingers will always give people the wrong impression (unless you're *very* strange).

Straightening a man's tie is an invitation to have your bum pinched.

Only ever feed people who you would like to be fed by.

OFFICE SEXUAL RELATIONS

Keep dates with workmates a secret until you're married.

Never assume your older work mates consider you too young to flirt with.

Orchestrate over-night trips to conventions with cute workmates.

All rules are invalid once in the pub.

THE LITTLE BOOK OF OFFICE BOLLOCKS

What the Drinks Machine Says About You...

Like deducing quirks and foibles from the clothes people wear in the office, so the choices your co-workers make at the drinks' machine can be very revealing.

Strong black coffee: This person is stressed or recovering from a big night out. Drink this to give the impression that you work really hard.

WHAT THE DRINKS MACHINE SAYS ABOUT YOU

Regular white coffee: The person who drinks white coffee is trying to give the same impression as the hardworking black coffee person, but is actually quite happy. A white-coffee drinker wants to be in *Friends* and enjoys saying 'latte' and other foreign sounding words.

***Black tea**:* Anyone who drinks tea black must be vaguely religious and well-travelled, or else a super-sick lacto-intolerant person.

***White tea**:* Ah, the salt of the earth kind. Likes watching TV soaps set in the North; Dad was a builder; enjoys reading tabloid newspapers.

WHAT THE DRINKS MACHINE SAYS ABOUT YOU

Hot chocolate: This person is decadent, seductive and hedonistic. Or else they're on a diet and trying not to actually *eat* real chocolate. Or maybe they just can't handle caffeine anymore.

Diet Coke: Choosing Diet Coke indicates someone from the Bridget Jones generation seeking half-naked builders. A calorie-counter.

THE LITTLE BOOK OF OFFICE BOLLOCKS

Sugary fizzy drinks: Likely to be a slightly infantile IT person looking for a cheap rush. Wants to be Tango'd.

Vegetable soup: Warning! This person is very strange.

WHAT THE DRINKS MACHINE SAYS ABOUT YOU

Still mineral water: This person is a very pious health freak trying to appear like a model. Or maybe they're just trying to clear up spots.

Sparkling mineral water: Same as the still water but with assumed extra sophistication. Probably went on a school exchange to France.

THE LITTLE BOOK OF OFFICE BOLLOCKS

When it's Time to Find Another Job

OK, so you've finally had enough. You don't want to end up like Norman the Techie who's been at the company for ninety-five years. If all that valuable experience, plus a book token and a pint after work as a send-off isn't enough to take away from your office job, here are a few tips.

Steal as much as possible from the stationery cupboard.

WHEN IT'S TIME TO FIND ANOTHER JOB

Save your newly updated CV as 'Work for next week.doc' on your computer.

Use office time to trawl internet job sites.

Create a file somewhere on the network called 'ie54_WP' to hide all the files you don't want other people to look at.

THE LITTLE BOOK OF OFFICE BOLLOCKS

Take responsibility for long-term projects you know you won't be around to complete.

Fabricate a chronic illness for multiple doctor appointments to cover interview days.

Hang out with the people in the post room so you can send job applications for free. If you have no post room, offer to do the postal run so you can post all your CVs free of charge (no one counts the amounts of stamps purchased on a receipt).

WHEN IT'S TIME TO FIND ANOTHER JOB

Send 'Hope you're well' e-mails to previous employers in advance of reference requests.

Suggest a sweep-stake on who will be the next person to leave the office.

Campaign for a team-building day in order to extract one final night-out on the boss.

THE LITTLE BOOK OF OFFICE BOLLOCKS

Lobby the management for broadband internet access so you can watch live sports online with greater ease.

Sabotage your computer by deleting all files which end in *.dll* to swing an extended break while the incompetent IT people try and fix it.

Have sex with as many people in the office as possible, safe in the knowledge that you won't have to live with the fall-out for too long.

WHEN IT'S TIME TO FIND ANOTHER JOB

Create a false e-mail address and use it as referee so you can write your own reference without anyone in the office knowing you are leaving or being able to say anything bad about you.

Gather as much sensitive material from the office records as possible and offer it to your potential employer.

THE LITTLE BOOK OF OFFICE BOLLOCKS

Announce that you're about to get married and rake in all the gifts – they'll never know you didn't do it!

Get an internet sales job to do on the side during office hours.

Undertake charity events. Canvas all your co-workers to sponsor you and then keep all the money (this can actually be done at any time).

WHEN IT'S TIME TO FIND ANOTHER JOB

Try and leave just after, rather than before, your birthday in an attempt to maximise your gift potential.

Sign your most annoying co-workers up for mass e-mails and porn sites so that they are inundated with spam after you've left.

Write anonymous letters to your co-workers telling them of all the things that are said about them behind their backs.

THE LITTLE BOOK OF OFFICE BOLLOCKS

Complain that the stockroom is in a shocking mess and that you need a day or two to tidy it up. Do it fast and then kick back for the rest of the time with a good book.

Fabricate a crisis in your house, such as faulty plumbing or wiring. All those days spent supervising workmen who are there to make your home habitable can be spent going to interviews.

WHEN IT'S TIME TO FIND ANOTHER JOB

Plant damaging typos into letters which make the boss look stupid and incompetent.

Fabricate a pregnancy. If you are a woman this means inevitable time off. If you are a man it means you can get away with being stressed without anyone else commenting on it.

THE LITTLE BOOK OF OFFICE BOLLOCKS

Surf dubious websites on your enemy co-workers' computers and then inform IT that you think internet privileges are being abused (make sure your own cache is clean first).

Release lots of bugs on a Monday so that the office needs to be fumigated, producing a cunning day off.

WHEN IT'S TIME TO FIND ANOTHER JOB

Start a rumour campaign about people who annoy you through graffiti in the office toilet.

Drop stink bombs for early closing on Fridays.

THE LITTLE BOOK OF OFFICE BOLLOCKS

How to Get the Sack

If you can't be bothered to work out your letter of resignation, why not go out with a bang?

Suggest a paint-ball day out and repeatedly shoot the boss.

Pirate CDs and software on the office CD-burner and sell them on street corners during lunchtimes.

HOW TO GET THE SACK

Suggest a conker tournament and accidentally wrap the knuckles of all the managers. Tell them they lost despite the fact they soaked their conkers in vinegar.

Sell all the office's highlighter pens to the kids at the local school.

Steal tea-bags and loo-rolls from the store cupboard.

Repeatedly leave whoopie cushions on your manager's chair.

HOW TO GET THE SACK

Implement a 'buy one get one free' day without consulting the boss.

Stop washing and allow your dirty underwear to build up in a pile under your desk.

Demand the right to speak backwards (sdrawkcab kaeps ot thgir eht dnameD).

Seduce your boss's spouse and then leave the Polaroids on your desk for all to see.

HOW TO GET THE SACK

Start wearing the same clothes as your boss, follow them home at night and wait on their doorstep until morning.

Develop fake multiple personalities including one that can't help kicking people on higher grades.

Refuse to come into work because you have developed an allergy to office bollocks.

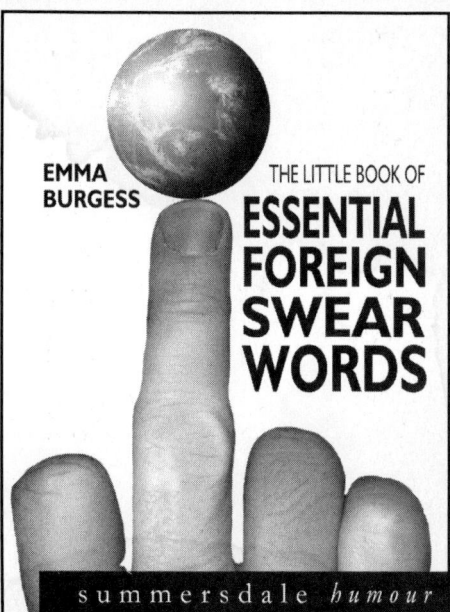

EMMA BURGESS

THE LITTLE BOOK OF ESSENTIAL FOREIGN SWEAR WORDS

summersdale *humour*

For the latest humour books from
Summersdale, check out

www.summersdale.com